The Positivity Switch

PRACTICAL STEPS TO A HAPPIER YOU

by Nuria Corbi

This book is intended to inspire and guide you on your journey toward a more positive and fulfilling life. While I've shared personal stories, insights, and practical suggestions, it's important to remember that everyone's journey is unique. The ideas and exercises in this book are not a substitute for professional advice, whether medical, psychological, or otherwise.

If you're dealing with significant challenges or concerns, I encourage you to seek support from a qualified professional. The strategies in this book are meant to complement your personal growth journey, not replace expert guidance.

Finally, while I believe in the power of positivity, please know that there's no such thing as a one-size-fits-all approach to life. Take what resonates, adapt it to your own needs, and remember to be kind to yourself along the way. After all, life is about progress, not perfection.

1st edition 2024

ISBN 978-1-7394865-4-9

Homeboss Media

About the Author

Nuria Corbi is an entrepreneur, writer, and self-publishing enthusiast who firmly believes in the power of positivity – and a good cup of coffee.

Born in Spain, raised in Germany, and happily settled in the UK, Nuria's career path has been as varied as the British weather, spanning graphic design, language teaching, and even running a bakery.

Since discovering self-publishing in 2019, Nuria has shared her knowledge through her popular YouTube channel, The Home Boss, where she inspires others to turn their creative dreams into thriving businesses.

She's also an award-winning children's book author and the creator of a much-loved Children's Book Course, helping countless students bring their stories to life.

In The Positivity Switch, Nuria blends her life lessons with practical insights to help readers embrace joy, clarity, and resilience.

When she's not writing or teaching, you'll find her on the Essex coast or in London, juggling gardening tools, good books, and great coffee – sometimes all at once.

Contents

Dedication   VII

Introduction   1

1. The Appreciation Switch   9

2. The Mindfulness Switch   16

3. The Visualisation Switch   25

4. The Kindness Switch   32

5. The Self-Belief Switch   40

6. The Perspective Switch   49

7. The Resilience Switch   56

8. The Practice of Positivity   62

9. When the Lights Go Dim   68

10. The Final Switch: Your Life's Light   74

11. The Science Behind Positivity: It's Not Just   80
     Fluff

12. Overcoming Challenges   87

13. The Seven Switches: Quick Wins and Simple   94
     Tips

14. Cheat Sheet for Switching On Positivity   99

15. Bonus Section: Staying Positive in a Divided   103
     World

16. Shine on: Over to you   110

17. What Next?   114

To all those people who keep shining even when the clouds
roll in.

You know who you are.

Introduction

The Positivity Switch

Welcome to The Positivity Switch! I'm Nuria Corbi, and I'm genuinely excited to have you here. Let's face it, life isn't always sunshine and rainbows – sometimes it can be a real struggle. But I've learned that even in the craziest moments, there's a way to flip your mindset and find a little light. That's what this book is all about.

Over the years, I've explored many paths; teaching languages in sunny Spain, running a bakery, dabbling in online businesses like a jewellery store and a gardening blog, and eventually finding my groove as a self-publisher on Amazon KDP since 2019. Each of these adventures brought its share of triumphs, challenges, and yes, a few "what was I thinking?" moments.

Through it all, one truth kept shining through: positivity changes everything. It's not about ignoring the hard stuff or pretending life's a fairy tale. It's about flicking those mental switches that help us see possibilities instead of problems, light instead of shadows, and opportunities instead of obstacles.

You might already know me from my YouTube channel, The Home Boss, where I show people how to turn creative ideas into thriving businesses (and occasionally overshare about my love of coffee). Whether you're a regular viewer or we're meeting for the first time, I'm thrilled to share this journey with you.

Why Positivity Matters

Let's be real – life loves to throw us curveballs. Maybe you've faced setbacks, disappointments, or those days when it feels like even your coffee machine is conspiring against you. I've been there. But here's the thing: the way we think shapes the way we live.

Positivity isn't about slapping on a fake smile and pretending everything's fine. It's about learning to focus on the good, even when life feels overwhelmingly difficult. It's about saying, "Okay, this is hard, but what can I do about it?" It's about shifting your mindset to find strength, clarity, and yes, maybe even a little joy, even in the tough moments.

A Little About My Journey

For as long as I can remember, I've been fascinated by the power of thoughts. Growing up, I was always encouraged to look on the bright side – sometimes to the point where I'd think, *Okay, but can I just complain for a second*? But those lessons stuck with me.

When I started self-publishing, I quickly realised that it wasn't all unicorns and glitter. There were skills to learn, setbacks to navigate, and plenty of self-doubt whispering, "Are you sure you can do this?" But instead of focusing on what I didn't know, I decided to focus on what I could do – and slowly, things started falling into place.

That's the heart of this book: sharing the mindset shifts that helped me along the way, so you can create your own path to positivity, no matter where you're starting from.

Introducing the Seven Switches

At some point, I started thinking of these mindset shifts as "switches." Kind of like flicking on a light in a dark room – suddenly, everything looks clearer. Here are the seven switches we'll explore together:

1. The Appreciation Switch: Learning to notice and value the good in your life, big or small.

2. The Mindfulness Switch: Being present in the moment instead of getting caught up in worries.

3. The Kindness Switch: Extending kindness to yourself and others, even when it's tough.

4. The Self-Belief Switch: Building confidence in yourself, one small step at a time.

5. The Perspective Switch: Shifting how you view challenges and finding opportunities in setbacks.

6. The Resilience Switch: Bouncing back from difficulties with strength and determination.

7. The Visualisation Switch: Using the power of your imagination to shape your future.

Each of these switches represents a simple yet powerful way to bring more positivity into your life. They're practical, relatable, and grounded in real-life experiences – because, let's be honest, we don't have time for fluff.

Why These Switches Matter

Why these seven? Because they reflect the areas where positivity can have the biggest impact. When you practice appreciation, it's easier to shift your perspective. When you strengthen your self-belief, bouncing back from setbacks feels less daunting. These switches aren't magic wands – they're tools for creating real, lasting changes in how you approach life.

The Impact Positivity Can Have on Your Life

Positivity doesn't just change how we feel – it changes how we live. When we focus on the good, we start to see opportunities instead of obstacles. We build stronger relationships, manage stress more effectively, and approach challenges with a sense of possibility instead of defeat.

This book isn't about being positive every single moment (because honestly, who can do that?). It's about learning to flick the switches that bring more joy, clarity, and strength into your life.

A Conversation, Not a Lecture

I want this book to feel like a chat with a good friend – the kind where you can laugh, vent, and walk away feeling a little lighter. No judgement, just encouragement and practical ideas to help you navigate life's ups and downs. My hope is that by the end of this book, you'll feel inspired, empowered, and ready to flick your own positivity switch whenever you need it.

With love,

Nuria

CHAPTER ONE

The Appreciation Switch

I can't say I ever made a deliberate decision to reflect on the positives in my life – it's just something I've always done. Looking back, I realise that my upbringing gently nudged me in this direction. My family wasn't particularly religious, but we were big on noticing the good things in life. At school, this was reinforced during religious studies. To this day, I can't remember much about those lessons, but I do remember the focus on gratitude.

Over time, I noticed I had a peculiar habit: at the end of each day, I'd naturally reflect on what had gone well. It wasn't some grand epiphany or part of a motivational routine – I simply found myself thinking about the small things that made me smile. Maybe it was a kind word, a completed task, or just a moment of peace with a cup of tea. These reflections weren't earth-shattering, but they quietly shaped how I saw the world.

Discovering Appreciation

Years later, I came across Esther Hicks, renowned for her teachings on the Law of Attraction, and heard her explain the difference between gratitude and appreciation - it was as if someone had switched on a light in my mind. She described gratitude as being tied to external benefits – what you're thankful to have or experience – while appreciation digs deeper, focusing on the essence of something or someone. It's the difference between saying, "Thank goodness for coffee," and truly savouring the warmth, aroma, and first sip of your morning brew.

Without realising it, I'd made this shift myself. My reflections had evolved from gratitude for the obvious big things to appreciating life's smaller details: the way sunlight streams through a window, the crisp satisfaction of ticking off a task, or the rare joy of a perfectly ripe avocado. This is why I call it The Appreciation Switch. It's not a complicated technique or a daily chore – it's a mindset shift. It's about training your brain to notice the good, even on days when the good feels like it's hiding. Think of it as an internal treasure hunt, where even finding the smallest nugget of joy counts as a win.

Flicking the Appreciation Switch

If you're thinking, "That's great, but I'm not wired like that," don't worry – it's a learnable skill. Start small. At the end of the day, find one thing that made you smile, one thing you accomplished, or one thing you're glad to have in your life. It could be as simple as, "I made it through Monday without crying into my coffee." Over time, this quiet practice can become second nature, like an invisible shift that helps you end the day on a lighter note.

Here's the thing about appreciating peace: we often don't realise how precious it is until it's gone. Life's calm moments – uneventful evenings, small victories, or even a traffic-free commute – can seem ordinary at the time, but they're often the ones we miss the most when things get tough.

A Humbling Lesson

I once heard a conversation that really stuck with me. A friend's husband had a rare Sunday afternoon with no plans – no meetings, no deadlines, no obligations. Instead of enjoying the peace, he spent the day scrolling on his phone, restless and wishing for something more exciting. Fast-forward a month, and he found himself knee-deep in a work crisis, running on fumes. He later admitted to my friend that he thought back to that quiet Sunday and realised what a gift it was. Since then, he's made a point to savour little moments of calm, like his morning coffee or a quick walk during lunch. Those moments became his lifeline during stressful times, and honestly, I could relate.

Why Appreciation Matters

Stories like this remind me that appreciation isn't about waiting for life to hand you grand, Instagram-worthy moments. It's about noticing the small joys that fill our days, like a quiet evening, a friendly smile, or the warmth of a perfectly brewed cup of tea.

Exercises to Practice Appreciation

Daily Appreciation Log:

- At the end of the day, jot down three things you appreciated.

- Reflect on why each one mattered.

- Look for patterns – what brings you joy most consistently?

Task:

Once a week, share your appreciation with someone who contributed to your positive moment. It could be a quick text, a handwritten note, or just a heartfelt "thank you."

> **Quote:** "Enjoy the little things; for one day you may look back and realise they were the big things." — Robert Brault

This quote reminds us that the most meaningful moments often come from the small, everyday experiences we overlook.

Taking time to appreciate life's little moments is transformative – it can shift your entire outlook. But have you ever found yourself so caught up in the rush of life that even the most beautiful moments pass you by? That's where mindfulness comes in. Let's explore how staying present can help you fully absorb the moments you're learning to appreciate.

CHAPTER TWO

The Mindfulness Switch

Have you ever realised just how much of your day is spent thinking about things that have already happened – or worrying about things that haven't? It's astonishing, really, how much mental real estate we give to thoughts that pull us away from the present moment. For me, mindfulness wasn't something I actively practiced at first. It started with small, quiet moments – pausing to notice the way sunlight filtered through a window or taking an extra minute to watch the birds in my garden.

Over time, I realised these tiny pauses had a remarkable effect. They brought me back to the present, quieted the mental chatter, and helped me feel more grounded. Little did I know, those small moments of awareness were the beginning of a shift in how I approached life.

A Question That Shifted Everything

Mindfulness has always felt somewhat second nature to me, but I distinctly remember a moment that cemented its importance. I was going through a particularly stressful time, feeling consumed by worry, when I stopped and asked myself, Will this problem matter in 10 years – or even 5? It was like flicking a mental switch. Suddenly, I could see how much energy I was wasting on something that likely wouldn't leave a lasting mark on my life. That one question helped me let go of some of the stress and come back to the present.

Another thought that has helped me in moments of worry is this: What has changed since yesterday? What is worse today than it was yesterday? Nine times out of ten, the answer is "nothing." The only thing that had changed was the amount of energy I was giving to my worries. Recognising this helped me take a step back and regain a sense of calm.

Later, I realised that living in the moment isn't just important – it's essential. A teacher of mine once said, "The past is history, the future is a mystery, and the present is a gift." That line stayed with me because it's a simple but profound truth: the present moment is the only one we truly have.

Introducing The Mindfulness Switch

Mindfulness, to me, is like hitting the "pause" button on life. It's a way of saying, "Hang on a second – this moment matters." I call it The Mindfulness Switch because it's something you can consciously choose to turn on whenever you feel overwhelmed or distracted. And no, it doesn't require hours of meditation or becoming a zen master. It starts with the smallest moments of awareness.

When my children were little, I had a poem stuck to my fridge door with a magnet. It read:

"Cleaning and scrubbing can wait till tomorrow,

For babies grow up, we've learned to our sorrow.

So quiet down cobwebs, dust go to sleep,

I'm rocking my baby, and babies don't keep!"

At the time, it was a gentle reminder to slow down and savour the moments with my little ones. There was always something that needed doing – cleaning, errands, work – but the poem reminded me that those tasks could wait. What truly mattered were the fleeting moments of rocking my babies to sleep, hearing their giggles, or watching their curiosity unfold.

Now that my children are grown, I understand even more deeply how true that message was. Those moments we think of as "ordinary" – a bedtime story, a shared laugh, or even just sitting together – are the ones that stay with us.

A Powerful Reminder

A friend of mine shared a story about her husband, James, who always seemed to be juggling a million things. One evening, as he worked late in his home office, he overheard their young daughter laughing in the next room. Something about her laughter made him pause. He left his desk and found her building a pillow fort, her face glowing with excitement.

For a moment, James thought about going back to work – deadlines loomed, after all. But instead, he stayed. They spent hours building the fort, laughing, and telling stories. Later that night, as he tucked her into bed, James admitted to my friend that this moment was far more valuable than anything else he could have done that evening. From then on, he made a conscious effort to set aside time each day to be fully present with his family.

Stories like this remind us how easy it is to let life's busyness pull us away from the present moment. But they also show us the power of pausing, refocusing, and truly connecting with what's happening right now.

Flicking The Mindfulness Switch

Mindfulness isn't about clearing your mind completely – it's about becoming aware of the moment you're in and embracing it fully. Here are a few ways to start:

Exercise: The 5-Senses Reset

- Pause wherever you are and take a deep breath.

- Notice five things you can see.

- Notice four things you can touch.

- Notice three things you can hear.

- Notice two things you can smell.

- Notice one thing you can taste.

This quick exercise pulls you out of your thoughts and into the present moment.

Exercise: Five-Minute Focus

Set a timer for five minutes.

Choose one thing to focus on (e.g., your breathing, a tree outside, or the sounds around you).

When your mind wanders, gently bring it back to your focus.

Task:

Choose one routine activity (like brushing your teeth or drinking your morning coffee) to practice mindfully for a week. Pay attention to every sensation and step involved.

Finding Joy in the Now

Mindfulness isn't about trying to control everything or making every moment perfect. It's about noticing the little things that bring you peace and joy right now. When you flick The Mindfulness Switch, you're giving yourself permission to slow down and fully live in the moment.

Quote:

> "Do not dwell in the past, do not dream of the future, concentrate the mind on the present moment."
> — Buddha

Buddha's wisdom reminds us that life is happening right now. By anchoring ourselves in the present, we open the door to clarity, peace, and connection.

By now, you've started to explore the power of mindfulness – how being present in the moment can help you find clarity, peace, and connection. But what if we could take that sense of focus and use it to shape the future we want?

Mindfulness anchors us in the here and now, but visualisation helps us look ahead with intention and imagination. It's not just about daydreaming (although that can be fun too); it's about creating a vivid picture of what you want and aligning your actions to make it a reality.

Think of it as building a mental roadmap – one where every detail you envision helps you take the next step towards your goals. Whether it's a career change, a dream home, or simply finding more joy in your daily life, The Visualisation Switch will show you how to harness the power of your imagination to create a future that excites and inspires you.

So, let's dive into the next chapter and discover how to turn your dreams into something tangible and achievable.

CHAPTER THREE

The Visualisation Switch

Have you ever caught yourself daydreaming about something wonderful – a dream home, a career goal, or just a perfectly quiet Sunday morning with no emails, no laundry, and no interruptions? (Bliss, right?) If you have, congratulations – you've already dabbled in visualisation. The good news is, you're a natural. The even better news? You can turn this habit into a powerful tool for shaping your future.

For me, visualisation didn't start as a deliberate practice. It was more like an accidental hobby. As a child, I often imagined what my future might look like – where I'd live, what I'd do, and what kind of life I'd create. What I didn't realise at the time was how much those daydreams were shaping my choices and, eventually, my reality.

Personal Reflections: Dreams with a Dash of Reality

When I was younger, I often daydreamed about owning my own house with a garden. In my mind, it was perfect – a little patch of green heaven with flowers, maybe a swing, and a cosy home to call my own. The funny thing is, I wasn't exactly focused on making it happen. My visualisation wasn't particularly detailed or intentional, but I returned to it often, letting the image play out in my mind.

Years later, when I finally got that house and garden, I realised just how much that dream had guided me. Visualisation, even when it wasn't structured or conscious, helped me focus on what I truly wanted and take the steps to make it happen.

Of course, life doesn't always deliver exactly what you imagine. Sometimes it gives you a slightly different version – one you might not have even considered – but one that turns out to be just what you needed. I've experienced this with my business as well. I always visualised working for myself, but my early ideas of what that looked like were vague and, frankly, a bit off the mark. It wasn't until

I really focused on what I wanted that things started to align. Visualisation helped me clarify my goals and take actionable steps to achieve them.

The Visualisation Switch

So, what exactly is The Visualisation Switch? It's about harnessing the natural power of your imagination to create a clear picture of what you want. This isn't just about wishful thinking – it's about using visualisation as a tool to align your thoughts, intentions, and actions.

Think of your mind as a GPS system. If you don't input a destination, it'll take you on a meandering journey to who-knows-where. But if you're clear about where you want to go, your brain starts working out how to get you there. That's the magic of visualisation – it gives your mind a map to follow.

The Struggle with Perfection

Now, I'd love to tell you that I've always been a visualisation pro, but the truth is, I often struggled with overthinking. I wanted my visualisations to be perfect. I'd get caught up in tiny details, trying to make everything just right in my mind. The result? Paralysis. Instead of moving forward, I'd be stuck, worrying that my vision wasn't "good enough."

What I've learned is this: you don't have to get it perfect. Your vision doesn't need to be a Hollywood blockbuster with a flawless script. It just needs to be clear enough to guide you. Start where you are, do your best, and trust that the process will unfold. As with anything, practice makes perfect – or at least, *progress*.

Flicking The Visualisation Switch

Here's the beauty of visualisation: it doesn't require special tools, a fancy setup, or hours of free time. It just requires your imagination and a willingness to dream. Here are some practical ways to flick the switch:

Exercise: Create a Mental Movie

- Close your eyes and imagine a goal you'd like to achieve.

- Picture it as if it's already happened. What does it look like? How does it feel?

- Add details – where are you? Who's with you? What's around you?

- Let yourself really soak in the experience for a few minutes.

Exercise: Vision Boards

- Gather some old magazines, printouts, or Pinterest images that represent your goals.

- Create a vision board (physical or digital) to help bring your visualisations to life.

- Place it somewhere you'll see it daily, like your workspace or phone wallpaper.

Task:

- Write down your goals and visualise yourself achieving them. Be specific – include the emotions, the setting, and the little details.

Seeing Is Believing

Visualisation isn't about wishful thinking; it's about connecting your dreams to your actions. When you create a vivid picture of what you want, you give your brain a clear target to work towards. It's like planting a seed in your mind and watching it grow.

Quote:

> "Go confidently in the direction of your dreams. Live the life you have imagined." – Henry David Thoreau

Thoreau's words remind us that visualisation is the first step to living the life we desire. It's about seeing the possibilities and daring to believe in them.

Visualisation helps us create a vivid mental roadmap for our dreams, turning possibilities into plans and plans into reality. But here's the thing: sometimes, the best way to make progress isn't by focusing inward, but by looking outward.

Kindness has a unique way of shifting our perspective. It reminds us that we're all connected and that even the smallest acts of compassion can have a profound impact. Whether it's offering a helping hand or sharing a kind word, kindness has the power to brighten someone's day – and your own.

Let's explore how flicking The Kindness Switch can transform not just your outlook but the world around you.

CHAPTER FOUR

The Kindness Switch

Have you ever noticed how a simple act of kindness can instantly brighten your day? Whether you're the one giving it or the one receiving it, kindness has this magical way of shifting focus away from stress and negativity. It's like flicking a switch that redirects your energy from "Ugh, this is awful" to "Okay, maybe the world isn't so bad after all."

For me, helping someone else is one of the quickest ways to break free from my own worries. It doesn't have to be grand – sometimes, it's as simple as holding the door open for someone or offering a genuine smile. Kindness is a bit like confetti: it costs almost nothing, but it has the power to brighten up everything around it.

Why Kindness Matters

Kindness is something I value above all else. To me, a kind person is always beautiful. In fact, I often find myself (unintentionally) judging people by how kind they are. It's not the fairest measuring stick, I'll admit, but kindness is the quality I hold in the highest regard. And I firmly believe that if I want to receive kindness from others, I should give kindness in abundance.

The ripple effect of kindness is extraordinary. It doesn't just help the person on the receiving end; it lifts your own spirits too. It's like a boomerang – you throw it out there, and somehow, it always comes back.

The Power of Helping Someone Else

There have been times in my life when I've been stuck in a worry spiral, unable to think my way out of a problem. You know those moments when your brain feels like it's running laps in a hamster wheel? In those times, I've discovered that helping someone else – even in a small way – has this magical ability to interrupt the cycle.

Whether it was lending a hand, offering a listening ear, or writing a thoughtful note, shifting my focus to someone else reminded me of the power of kindness. And, almost without fail, I found that in helping others, I also found clarity and calm in my own life.

I'll never forget one particular moment when I was weighed down by a major worry. I was standing in line for a taxi, completely lost in my own thoughts, when a lady getting into the taxi in front of me turned around and said,

"You know, your jacket is really beautiful; you look really nice."

Her words stopped me in my tracks. They didn't solve the problem I was facing, but they struck me deeply. I've always wondered if she sensed the heaviness I was carrying and decided to share a moment of kindness to lift my spirits. Whatever her reason, that small gesture stayed with me, reminding me of the profound impact kindness can have.

Over time, I've realised that kindness isn't just about offering compliments or grand gestures – it's also about extending understanding to others, even when they're being, well... a bit difficult.

Take the cashier I encountered one particularly rough day. My coffee had spilled over my blouse at work, my bus home was late, and I still had to buy groceries for our dinner. By the time I got to the checkout, I was ready to snap. The cashier barely looked up, her demeanor distant and unhelpful.

But instead of letting my frustration take over, I paused and thought, *Maybe she's having a rough day too.* So, I smiled and said, "Thank you for your help – I hope you have a good evening." Her whole face lit up. She smiled back and even apologised for being distracted. I left the store feeling lighter, realising that my small act of kindness hadn't just shifted her mood – it had transformed mine too.

Flicking The Kindness Switch

Kindness is a gift that grows the more you share it. Here are a few simple ways to flip The Kindness Switch and make it a daily practice:

Exercise: Small Acts, Big Impact

- Perform one act of kindness each day, no matter how small.

- Write down what you did and how it made you feel.

- Notice how your kindness inspires others – track the ripples it creates.

Task:

- Commit to helping someone in your community, whether it's volunteering, mentoring, or offering support to a friend or neighbour.

Kindness as a Daily Practice

The more you practice kindness, the more natural it becomes. Flicking The Kindness Switch isn't about grand gestures; it's about finding small, everyday ways to create a positive impact. And the beauty of it is that as you give kindness, you'll find it coming back to you in unexpected and wonderful ways.

Quote:

> "No act of kindness, no matter how small, is ever wasted." — Aesop

Aesop's words remind us that even the smallest gesture can make a big difference. Kindness creates ripples that go far beyond the moment.

Kindness is a beautiful way to connect with the world, but it's also a reflection of something deeply personal: your belief in your ability to make a difference. That belief, when turned inward, becomes self-belief. How often do you doubt yourself or question whether you're capable? What would change if you trusted in your own potential? In the next chapter, we'll dive into The Self-Belief Switch and explore how to build confidence from the inside out.

CHAPTER FIVE

The Self-Belief Switch

Have you ever caught yourself saying, "I can't do this" or "I'm not good enough"? Self-doubt has this sneaky way of creeping in, just when we need confidence the most. But here's the thing: believing in yourself isn't about being perfect or having all the answers—it's about trusting that you can figure it out as you go.

I like to think of self-belief as a muscle. You're not born with it fully formed (and if you are, please tell me your secret!). It grows with every challenge you face, every goal you reach, and every time you surprise yourself by doing something you didn't think you could do.

Why Self-Belief Matters

Self-belief is the foundation for everything. It's the voice that says, "Go for it," even when the rest of your brain is coming up with a thousand reasons why you shouldn't. Without it, even the best opportunities can feel out of reach. With it, you start seeing challenges as adventures and setbacks as stepping stones.

From Doubt to Doing

I wasn't always brimming with self-belief – in fact, for most of my younger years, it was pretty much non-existent. But I noticed something interesting: whenever I was doing something I genuinely loved, my self-belief seemed to grow, almost without me realising it.

Take drawing, for example. As a child, I loved sketching and painting, and my dad encouraged me by teaching me how to use oil paints. His support gave me the confidence to keep going, even when my early attempts looked more like a toddler's finger painting than a masterpiece.

Another time in my life, long before I discovered self-publishing, I found myself facing a challenge that felt almost insurmountable: running a language school and teaching English as a foreign language. The thought of standing in front of a group of students made my palms sweat. My first class was with a small group of five, but to me, it felt like standing on stage at the Royal Albert Hall. My heart was racing, and I couldn't stop thinking, *What if I forget what to say? What if they stare at me blankly the whole time?*

As the lesson began, something surprising happened. I settled into the rhythm of teaching, and the nerves started to fade. The students were engaged, eager to learn, and their enthusiasm eased my own fears. By the end of the class, I wasn't just relieved – I was encouraged.

With each class I taught, my confidence grew. I went from trembling in front of a small group to feeling completely at ease teaching much larger classes. Looking back, I see that my initial fear wasn't a roadblock – it was an invitation to step out of my comfort zone.

Years later, I faced a different kind of challenge: writing a book. For years, I carried the dream of writing a book – like many people do. After all, don't we all have a book inside us, waiting to be written? But, as much as I loved the idea, I never really believed I could do it. Writing a book seemed like something reserved for "real" authors, not for someone like me.

Then one day, I stumbled across a YouTube channel that introduced me to the concept of publishing low-content books – planners, journals, that sort of thing. Intrigued, I thought, Why not give it a go? I published my first journal, and something incredible happened: I realised that publishing wasn't as unattainable as I'd imagined. I had learned the process, and for the first time, the idea of publishing a book with my own writing didn't feel so impossible.

That small step changed everything. Since then, I've not only published journals but also award-winning children's picture books. What once felt like a distant dream became achievable because I took that first leap and proved to myself that I could do it. The journey taught me something invaluable: self-belief doesn't always come first. Often, it grows with each small step you take, as you learn, try, and discover what you're truly capable of. What I learned from both experiences is that self-belief doesn't mean starting out fearless. It's about showing up, even when fear is screaming in your ear. Each small step you take builds your confidence, until one day, something that once felt impossible becomes second nature.

Later in life, I discovered that small successes had a way of boosting my self-belief, too. Every time I achieved something – even if it was just a tiny step forward – it gave me the courage to take on the next challenge.

Fast-forward to today, and my self-belief has grown to the point where I genuinely believe there's very little I can't do if I put my mind to it. It's not arrogance – it's a quiet confidence that comes from knowing I've faced challenges before and come out stronger.

The Self-Belief Switch

This is why I call it The Self-Belief Switch. It's not about waking up one day and suddenly feeling invincible (though wouldn't that be nice?). It's about flicking a mental switch that says, "I can handle this," even when you're not 100% sure how.

Building self-belief takes time, and it often starts with small, manageable steps. Each time you push yourself out of your comfort zone, you're strengthening that muscle. And before you know it, you'll find yourself tackling challenges you once thought were impossible.

Flicking The Self-Belief Switch

If you're not sure where to start, here are a few simple ways to flick The Self-Belief Switch and start building your confidence:

Exercise: A Success Journal

- At the end of each day, write down one thing you accomplished, no matter how small.

- Reflect on how it made you feel and what it says about your abilities.

Task:

- Think of something you've always wanted to try but have been too afraid to. Break it down into smaller, less intimidating steps, and take the first one this week.

Exercise: Positive Affirmations

- Write down three affirmations that resonate with you, such as "I am capable," "I learn from challenges," or "I deserve success."

- Repeat them to yourself daily, especially when self-doubt creeps in.

Trusting Yourself

Believing in yourself doesn't mean you'll never feel scared or unsure. It means trusting that you'll find a way forward, even when the path isn't clear. When you flip The Self-Belief Switch, you're giving yourself permission to take risks, embrace challenges, and grow into the person you're meant to be.

Quote:

> "Whether you think you can, or you think you can't—you're right." — Henry Ford

Henry Ford's words remind us that self-belief shapes our reality. When we believe in our potential, we create the foundation for success.

Self-belief is a powerful foundation, but life has a way of throwing us curveballs that can shake even the strongest confidence. That's where perspective comes in. Sometimes, the way we view a challenge makes all the difference. In the next chapter, we'll explore how to shift your perspective, find hidden opportunities, and turn setbacks into stepping stones.

CHAPTER SIX

The Perspective Switch

Perspective is one of those things that can completely transform how we experience life. Two people can look at the exact same situation and see two entirely different things – one sees a roadblock, and the other sees a detour that might lead to an even better destination. Over time, I've learned that how we choose to view our circumstances makes all the difference. Sometimes, all it takes is the tiniest tweak in perspective to turn a frustrating challenge into a valuable lesson or even a new opportunity.

Seeing the Bigger Picture

There have been countless times in my life when a shift in perspective changed everything. Take job applications, for example. Like most people, I've faced rejection. When I didn't get the jobs I applied for, it felt like a punch in the gut – a big, flashing sign that screamed failure. But as time went on, I started to notice a pattern. Each rejection was actually steering me toward something better – an opportunity I wouldn't have found otherwise. What felt like a dead end was really a shortcut to something more aligned with where I was meant to go.

The same goes for fitness goals. I've learned to celebrate small victories instead of obsessing over how far I still have to go. Whether it's going for a quick walk, stretching for 10 minutes, or just drinking an extra glass of water, I now see every small step as progress. Over time, those little actions add up to something far greater than an occasional big effort (and trust me, an "occasional big effort" used to be my go-to strategy).

Most recently, perspective came into play when we moved house. At first, I was reluctant – our old home was filled with memories, and I wasn't sure I could feel the same way about a new place. But as the dust settled (literally, after unpacking), I began to see how much positive change the move had brought to our lives. Shifting my perspective helped me embrace this new chapter and appreciate all the ways it made our lives better.

Introducing The Perspective Switch

Perspective, to me, is like looking out a window. Sometimes the glass is dirty or foggy, and everything outside seems bleak. But when you take a moment to clean the glass – or shift your angle – you start to see things more clearly. I call it The Perspective Switch because it's something you can choose to flick on by asking yourself key questions, like, *What's the lesson here?* or *How can I turn this into an opportunity?*

The Business That Built My Perspective

Years ago, my husband was working in a tough environment that wasn't doing his health any favours. I wanted to build a business that would allow us to work from home together. Full of determination, I started importing costume jewellery from the Far East and selling it on every platform I could think of – eBay, Amazon, Etsy, even my own website. I also sold at school fairs and Christmas markets.

For a while, things went well, but not well enough for my husband to leave his secure job. So, I pivoted. I started a blog called Sweet Life and Lemons, all about redesigning our garden on a budget. I gave myself a year to make it work. In hindsight, I can see that there were key things I didn't know about blogging back then, and it didn't bring the results I'd hoped for. At the time, I felt like all my efforts had been for nothing.

But looking back now, I realise those ventures weren't failures at all – they were stepping stones. Each one taught me something valuable: how to manage a business, how to stay determined, and how to keep learning. When I finally stumbled across low-content book publishing, it was like everything clicked into place. This time, I had the tools, the knowledge, and the experience I needed to succeed.

My self-publishing journey has been so fulfilling – it allowed my husband to leave his job, and now we work together, living the life we once dreamed of. Those earlier "failures" weren't failures at all. They were part of the path that led me to where I am today.

Flicking The Perspective Switch

Perspective isn't about ignoring challenges; it's about learning to see them in a different light. Here are some simple ways to practice flicking The Perspective Switch:

Exercise: The Silver Lining Challenge

- Think of a current challenge or frustration.

- Write down three potential positives or lessons that could come from it.

- Reflect on how these "silver linings" could guide your next steps.

Task:

- At the end of each day, write down one "silver lining" you noticed—even in small, ordinary moments.

- This practice helps you see possibilities instead of obstacles, even on the hardest days.

Choosing a New View

Flicking The Perspective Switch is about choosing to see the best in a situation, even when it's tough. It doesn't mean ignoring difficulties or pretending everything is perfect—it means recognising the power you have to reframe those difficulties. By shifting your perspective, you open yourself to new ideas, possibilities, and ways forward.

Quote:

> "We can complain because rose bushes have thorns, or rejoice because thorns have roses." — Alphonse Karr

This quote by Alphonse Karr perfectly illustrates how perspective shapes our experience. The facts don't change, but how we choose to see them makes all the difference.

Perspective helps us find meaning in challenges, but sometimes, meaning alone isn't enough. We need strength—the kind of quiet courage that keeps us standing when life feels relentless. That's where resilience comes in. In the next chapter, we'll explore how to build this inner strength so you can face life's storms with confidence and grace.

CHAPTER SEVEN

The Resilience Switch

Life has a way of testing us, doesn't it? Just when you think you've got everything under control, along comes one of life's surprises. Resilience is what keeps us going when the going gets tough. It's not about avoiding challenges or pretending everything's fine when it's not. It's about bouncing back, dusting yourself off, and saying, "Okay, life, is that all you've got?"

The truth is, resilience isn't something we're born with – it's something we build, brick by brick, through life's ups and downs. And let's face it, most of us have had plenty of opportunities to practice.

Why Resilience Matters

There's a quiet power in resilience. It's what allows us to keep moving forward, even when we feel like standing still. Over the years, I've learned that resilience doesn't mean thriving in every moment. Sometimes, it's simply about surviving—putting one foot in front of the other until things feel manageable again. And you know what? That's okay.

Finding Strength in the Storms

My life hasn't been a smooth, sunny stroll through the park. It's been more like hiking up a mountain in unpredictable weather – beautiful at times, but also exhausting and occasionally muddy. There have been countless moments that tested my resilience, from small setbacks to challenges that felt overwhelming.

What I've learned is that resilience isn't about never falling. It's about always rising – stronger, wiser, and maybe a little muddier than before. For example, when life handed me one of its infamous curveballs, I'd often find myself thinking, This is it. This is the thing that's going to do me in. And yet, here I am, still standing.

The Silver Linings

The funny thing about resilience is that it often reveals its value after the fact. Take setbacks, for instance. At the time, they can feel like the end of the world. But looking back, I've realised that those challenges often carried lessons or opportunities I wouldn't have found otherwise.

Take moving house, for example. I loved my old home and was reluctant to leave, but the move ended up being one of the best things for us. Shifting my perspective allowed me to see the positive changes it brought, and resilience helped me embrace the transition. It wasn't easy, but it was worth it.

Introducing The Resilience Switch

Resilience, to me, is like a tree standing tall in a storm. Its roots keep it grounded, its branches may bend, but it rarely breaks. I call this The Resilience Switch because it's something you can choose to turn on by tapping into your inner strength and reminding yourself of the challenges you've already overcome. Each storm you weather makes you stronger for the next one.

Balancing Strength with Kindness

Now, let's address that well-worn phrase, "What doesn't kill us makes us stronger." While it's true, it's also important to remember that we're not robots. Resilience isn't about ploughing through life without a second thought—it's about finding balance.

During the tough times, yes, we gather strength. But the quiet moments, the times when life feels calm and manageable, are just as important. Those are the moments to recharge, to appreciate, and to prepare for whatever comes next.

Flipping The Resilience Switch

Resilience isn't something you switch on and off like a lightbulb—it's more like a dimmer switch. Some days it's brighter, and some days it's barely flickering, but it's always there. Here are a couple of simple ways to strengthen your resilience:

Exercise: The Strength Inventory

- Think back to a time when you faced a tough challenge and came out the other side.

- Write down the strengths, skills, or resources you used to get through it.

- Keep this list as a reminder of your resilience for the next storm.

Task:

- Identify one area in your life where you've faced setbacks.

- Think about one small step you can take today to start moving forward again.

Building Resilience Every Day

Switching on The Resilience Switch isn't about being invincible—it's about being adaptable. It's about trusting yourself to weather the storms and remembering that each challenge you face builds your inner strength. And when life gives you a moment of calm, savour it. Those times of peace are what prepare us for the battles ahead.

Quote:

"The oak fought the wind and was broken, the willow bent when it must and survived." — Robert Jordan

Robert Jordan's words beautifully capture the essence of resilience. True strength isn't about never bending—it's about knowing when to adapt and trusting that you'll stand tall again.

CHAPTER EIGHT

The Practice of Positivity

LIVING THE POSITIVITY SWITCHES

Congratulations! You've made it through the seven switches, each one a tiny but mighty lever to shift your mindset and bring more joy, clarity, and resilience into your life. But now comes the real question: how do you make these switches a natural part of your daily routine?

Here's the thing – positivity isn't about plastering on a smile and pretending everything is fine (we all know that's exhausting). It's about learning to navigate life's ups and downs with a mindset that says, I've got this – or at least

I'll figure it out. And like any skill, positivity takes practice. The good news? Small, consistent steps can lead to lasting change.

The Power of the Seven Switches

If you've been paying attention—and I know you have—you've probably noticed how beautifully these switches work together. Appreciation helps you notice the good things, mindfulness grounds you in the moment, and visualisation keeps your eyes on the prize. Kindness connects you with others, self-belief reminds you how capable you are, perspective helps you see challenges in a new light, and resilience keeps you going when life feels like an obstacle course. Together, these switches form a simple yet powerful framework for positivity.

Making Positivity Part of Your Day

Here are a few ideas to keep the switches working for you:

1. Start Small

Rome wasn't built in a day, and neither is a positive mindset. Focus on one switch at a time. For example, dedicate a week to practicing The Appreciation Switch by jotting down three things you're grateful for each day. Once that feels as natural as scrolling Instagram, move on to the next switch.

2. Create Triggers

Pair each switch with something you already do daily. Brushing your teeth? Think of one kind act you can do that day. Sipping your morning coffee? Take five minutes to visualise a goal. These triggers make practicing positivity as automatic as turning on the kettle.

3. Reflect Weekly

At the end of each week, take a moment to look back. How did the switches affect your mood, relationships, or outlook? What came easily? What was a bit of a struggle?

These reflections are like a roadmap, guiding you as you deepen your practice.

The 30-Day Positivity Challenge

If you're ready to take things up a notch, I've got just the thing – a 30-day challenge to integrate all the switches into your life. Think of it as a month-long positivity boot camp (minus the yelling drill sergeant).

Week 1: The Appreciation Switch

Start small by noting three things you appreciate each day. Reflect on how this simple practice shifts your mood. Spoiler alert: it probably will.

Week 2: Add The Mindfulness Switch

Pair your gratitude practice with mindfulness by choosing one daily activity to do with full attention – whether it's eating a meal, taking a walk, or just breathing. Yes, breathing counts.

Week 3: Layer in The Visualisation and Kindness Switches

Spend five minutes each day visualising a goal, then commit to one act of kindness. Pay attention to how kindness connects you to others and how visualisation gives your actions a clear focus.

Week 4: Incorporate The Self-Belief, Perspective, and Resilience Switches

Each day, jot down a small win to boost your self-belief. Reframe one challenge using The Perspective Switch, and reflect on how past challenges have built your resilience.

By the end of this challenge, you'll have created a rock-solid foundation of positivity – one that will stick with you long after these 30 days.

Positivity as a Lifestyle

Positivity isn't about being happy all the time (because let's be real, nobody's that chipper). It's about equipping yourself with tools to face life with strength, clarity, and a little bit of grace. The more you practice the switches, the more natural they'll feel. Over time, positivity won't just be something you chase – it'll be a steady presence in your life.

Remember, this isn't about being perfect. Progress is the goal here. With each small step, you're building a life filled with purpose, joy, and resilience. And hey, if you stumble along the way, just flick The Perspective Switch and see it as part of the journey. You've got this.

CHAPTER NINE

When the Lights Go Dim

Let's be real – there will be days when flicking the positivity switches feels like trying to start a car with a dead battery. Life doesn't always stick to the script, or sometimes you just wake up feeling like a deflated balloon. And that's okay. These moments don't mean you've failed, and they certainly don't undo all the progress you've made. This chapter is your go-to guide for when positivity feels out of reach – a gentle nudge to help you find your way back to the light.

Recognising the Dim Moments

We've all been there: stuck in a spiral of stress, drained of energy, or just feeling plain "meh." Whether it's a tough day, a challenging season, or even a random low that you can't explain, the first step is to recognise how you're feeling – without beating yourself up for it. You're human, not a perpetual ray of sunshine, and bad days are part of the package. What matters is how you respond when the light dims.

Practical Strategies for Reconnecting

Here are a few simple tools to help you when the brightness seems out of reach. These aren't about forcing positivity – they're about gently creating space for it to reappear when it's ready.

1. Pause and Breathe

When everything feels overwhelming, take a timeout. Sit quietly, close your eyes, and focus on your breath. Inhale deeply, hold it for a few seconds, and exhale slowly. It's like hitting a reset button for your mind. Bonus points if you picture yourself blowing away stress like dandelion fluff.

2. Start Small

When the big picture feels too much, zoom in. Write down one thing you're grateful for, send a kind text to a friend, or drink a glass of water and think, I'm taking care of myself. These little steps may seem trivial, but they're like breadcrumbs leading you back to positivity.

3. Revisit the Switches

Think of the switches as old friends. Which one feels easiest to lean on right now? Maybe mindfulness feels too hard, but kindness feels doable. Or perhaps self-belief is hiding, but appreciation is just within reach. Start where you can – there's no wrong choice.

4. Seek Connection

Sometimes, the quickest way to lighten your load is to share it. Call a friend, text a family member, or chat with someone you trust. Letting someone else in on how you're feeling can be a powerful reminder that you're not alone. And who knows? They might offer a new perspective, a comforting word, or simply the warmth of their presence to help lift your spirits.

5. Be Gentle with Yourself

Here's your permission slip to take a break. Rest isn't laziness – it's fuel. Whether it's curling up with a book, taking a nap, or just sitting quietly, give yourself the space to recharge without guilt.

Reflecting on Resilience

Dim moments have a sneaky way of revealing our strength. Think back to a tough time you've faced in the past. What helped you through it? What strengths did you discover in yourself? These reflections are like a pep talk from your past self, reminding you that you've weathered storms before and can do it again.

A Compassionate Perspective

When positivity feels elusive, frustration can creep in. But instead of asking, *Why can't I stay positive?* try asking, *What do I need right now?* Maybe it's rest, maybe it's comfort, or maybe it's just a moment to breathe. This gentle shift in mindset opens the door to self-care and healing, making it easier to reconnect with your inner light.

Finding Light Again

Dim moments don't last forever. They're like passing clouds—they might block the sun for a while, but the light is still there, waiting to shine again. Positivity isn't about being cheerful all the time (that's exhausting). It's about trusting that the light will return, even when it feels distant.

So, when life feels heavy, take a deep breath, be kind to yourself, and remember: you have the tools to find your way back to the switches. And if all else fails, remind yourself of this simple truth: it's okay to be a work in progress.

CHAPTER TEN

The Final Switch: Your Life's Light

You've learned to flick seven transformative switches – each one designed to help you see the world a little brighter and bring more positivity into your life. But now we've arrived at the final switch, the one that ties everything together. This switch is all about you. It's the light you carry within, the unique energy and perspective only you can bring to the world. It's about realising that you have the power to shape not just your mindset, but your actions, your relationships, and ultimately, your life.

Taking Ownership of Your Mindset

Throughout this journey, the switches have been your toolkit – ways to unlock the incredible potential that's already inside you. The final switch is different. It's about stepping into that potential fully and owning it. It's about recognising that even when life feels dark, you can trust yourself to find the light again.

It's important to remember that the switches will work differently for everyone. We're all unique, with our own experiences, challenges, and perspectives that shape how we approach life. That's why your journey with these switches will look different from mine or anyone else's. And that's a good thing—because your light is entirely your own. The way you use these switches depends on your individual circumstances, strengths, and dreams.

This isn't about being relentlessly positive all the time (that's exhausting and, frankly, unrealistic). It's about knowing that no matter what happens, you have the tools to navigate life's twists and turns with strength, clarity, and intention. Your life's light is what makes your journey meaningful, and your unique approach is what makes it yours.

The Ripple Effect of Positivity

Here's the thing: your mindset doesn't just impact you—it radiates outward and touches everyone around you. When you choose appreciation, mindfulness, kindness, and resilience, you create ripples of positivity that inspire others to do the same.

Think about a time when someone's kindness or optimism lifted your spirits. Maybe it was a friend, a family member, or even a stranger. Now imagine how your own light could brighten someone else's day in the same way. When you switch on your switches, you're not just changing your life—you're contributing to a brighter, more connected world.

Practical Ways to Shine Your Light

Want to embrace and share your inner light? Start here:

1. Be Authentic

Let's ditch the idea of being perfect—it's overrated. Instead, let your true self shine, quirks and all. Positivity isn't about having it all together; it's about being real, showing up as you are, and embracing your imperfections.

2. Share Your Gratitude

Think of someone who's supported or inspired you and tell them how much they mean to you. It doesn't have to be fancy – a heartfelt thank-you can light up someone's day more than you realise.

3. Lead by Example

Positivity is contagious, but you don't need to preach about it. Simply live it. When others see how you handle challenges with grace, approach life with gratitude, or show kindness in tough situations, they'll feel inspired to do the same.

4. Celebrate Your Growth

Look at where you started and how far you've come. Celebrate the wins—big, small, and everything in between. You've done the work, and that deserves recognition.

Living with Purpose

Shining your light isn't about chasing perfection or achieving some ideal version of life. It's about living intentionally—choosing how you respond to challenges, how you connect with others, and how you nurture your own growth.

This final switch is a reminder that you are the author of your story. Every day is a blank page, and you have the power to write something beautiful, meaningful, and true to who you are.

Conclusion: Keep Switching on the Switches

As you close this book, take a moment to reflect on everything you've learned. The switches aren't just tools—they're a part of you now. They're always within reach, ready to guide you whenever you need them.

Keep activating those switches, keep shining your light, and trust that every small step you take is creating a brighter, more joyful life. You've had the power to change your mindset—and your world—all along. Now, go out there and live it.

The Science Behind Positivity: It's Not Just Fluff

Let's get one thing straight – positivity sometimes gets a bad rap. People hear the word and picture someone forcing a grin while their world crumbles around them. But here's the truth: positivity isn't about ignoring the tough stuff. It's about rewiring how we respond to it – and, believe it or not, there's science to back it up.

When we practice gratitude, mindfulness, kindness, or resilience, we're not just improving our mood. We're literally rewiring our brains and boosting our health. Who knew switching on these switches could be like hitting the jackpot for both your mind and body? Let's dive into the research behind why these switches work so well.

Gratitude: The Easy Win

Gratitude, or appreciation, is hands-down one of my favourite switches. Why? Because it's simple, and the rewards are huge.

Take this: a study by Emmons and McCullough found that people who kept a gratitude journal felt happier, had fewer headaches, and even slept better. That's right – jotting down "I'm thankful for my comfy socks" could lead to better sleep. Science is amazing, isn't it?

Here's how it works: gratitude shifts your focus. Instead of fixating on what's going wrong (hello, overdue bills), you start noticing what's going right (that nice cup of tea you had earlier). Over time, your brain gets better at spotting the good stuff – it's like training a positivity muscle. And the stronger it gets, the brighter your outlook becomes.

Mindfulness: Presence with a Purpose

When I first heard about mindfulness, I imagined I'd need to become a zen master, sitting cross-legged for hours while chanting "om." Thankfully, it turns out mindfulness can be way more practical (and less intimidating).

Research shows that mindfulness reduces stress and even lowers cortisol – the hormone responsible for making you feel like you're stuck in rush-hour traffic 24/7. A study by the American Psychological Association found that mindfulness-based practices can improve emotional regulation and ease anxiety.

The best part? Mindfulness is ridiculously simple to try. It's not about meditating for hours; it's about paying attention. Like really tasting your morning coffee instead of guzzling it in a daze. Or fully listening to a friend instead of planning your reply while they're still talking. Small moments, big impact.

Resilience: Your Superpower in Disguise

Resilience isn't just about "bouncing back." It's about bouncing forward. And, good news, it's something we can all build.

According to research by the American Psychological Association, resilience grows through things like supportive relationships, shifting your perspective, and building self-belief. Thanks to neuroplasticity – a fancy word for the brain's ability to adapt – every time we face a challenge, we're training ourselves to respond more effectively next time.

Think about it: each setback you've faced (and survived!) has quietly been preparing you for the next unexpected challenge life sends your way. It's like your brain is doing secret push-ups every time you dust yourself off and try again.

Positivity and Health: Science Says Yes

Here's the mind-blowing part: positivity isn't just good for your mood – it's good for your body too.

A Harvard study found that optimism is linked to a longer lifespan. We're talking about living longer and having a better shot at hitting 85 and still being the life of the party.

Positivity has been shown to boost immune function, reduce chronic pain, and even lower the risk of heart disease. It's like your body gives you a little "thank you" every time you choose to focus on the bright side.

Conclusion: Positivity with a Purpose

So, the next time someone rolls their eyes at "positivity," you can smile knowingly and say, "Actually, it's science." Gratitude rewires your focus, mindfulness grounds you in the present, resilience makes you stronger, and all of it together turns you into a healthier, happier human.

When you switch on these practices, you're not just brightening your day – you're investing in a better future for yourself. And that, my friend, is something worth smiling about.

References (Not Just Clickbait)

Gratitude and Well-Being:

Emmons, R. A., & McCullough, M. E. (2003). Counting Blessings Versus Burdens: An Experimental Investigation of Gratitude and Subjective Well-Being in Daily Life. Journal of Personality and Social Psychology.

URL: https://psycnet.apa.org/record/2003-09010-006

Mindfulness and Stress Reduction:

Chiesa, A., & Serretti, A. (2009). Mindfulness-Based Stress Reduction and Cortisol Awakening Response: A Systematic Review and Meta-Analysis. Psychoneuroendocrinology.

URL: https://www.sciencedirect.com/science/article/abs/pii/S0306453009000051

Resilience and Neuroplasticity:

American Psychological Association. Building Resilience in the Face of Challenges.

URL: https://www.apa.org/topics/resilience

Positivity and Longevity:

Lee, L. O., Kubzansky, L. D., & Kawachi, I. (2019). Optimism Is Associated with Exceptional Longevity in 2 Epidemiologic Cohorts of Men and Women. Proceedings of the National Academy of Sciences.

URL: https://www.pnas.org/content/116/37/18357

CHAPTER TWELVE

Overcoming Challenges

Staying positive can sometimes feel like trying to balance on a tightrope in a windstorm. Life has a way of keeping you on your toes – whether it's that unexpected bill, an overly critical comment, or simply a bad hair day. Let's just agree right now: struggling to stay upbeat doesn't mean you're failing; it means you're human.

Here's the thing: positivity isn't about slapping on a fake smile and pretending everything is fine. Positivity is about making small, intentional choices to shift your focus toward the good, even when the bad feels like it's taking over.

To do that, it helps to understand the obstacles standing in your way and how to outsmart them.

Negativity Bias: Blame It on Your Brain

Ever notice how one snarky comment can stick with you for days, but a dozen compliments barely register? That's your brain's negativity bias doing its thing – a survival trick leftover from when dodging saber-toothed tigers was a daily concern. Back then, noticing threats kept us alive. Now? It mostly keeps us awake at night replaying awkward conversations.

The good news? You can train your brain to stop fixating on the bad stuff. Gratitude is like a reset button for your mind. Every time you intentionally focus on something good, you're rewiring your brain to notice positivity more often. Think of it as strength training, but for your mindset – and no gym membership required.

Overwhelm and Stress: When Positivity Takes a Back Seat

Let's talk about stress. It's the uninvited guest that shows up, takes over the couch, and eats all your snacks. When you're overwhelmed, positivity feels like a distant memory, somewhere between "last summer's holiday" and "that time I had a full eight hours of sleep."

The trick? Create tiny pockets of calm. Take five minutes to breathe, stretch, or simply sit quietly without scrolling through your phone. Close your eyes, inhale deeply, and pretend you're on a sunny beach – or at least somewhere far away from your to-do list. Those small moments can help reset your brain, making space for a little positivity to sneak back in.

Criticism and Self-Doubt: That Inner Voice Needs a Timeout

We've all been there. Someone critiques your work, and suddenly your confidence crumbles like a poorly baked cake. Or worse, your own inner critic chimes in with a voice that sounds suspiciously like a grumpy version of yourself.

Here's a trick: reframe criticism as information. Ask yourself, Is this helpful? If it is, use it to improve. If it's not, toss it out like expired milk. And when it comes to that inner critic? Try talking to yourself as you would a friend. After all, you'd never tell your best mate, "*You're terrible at this, give up now,*" so why would you say it to yourself?

Lack of Support: When the World Feels Like a Wet Blanket

Being surrounded by negativity can feel like trying to swim upstream. Whether it's a toxic workplace, a challenging relationship, or just the general doom and gloom of the news, it's tough to keep your own positivity intact.

Here's where 'positivity anchors' come in. These are the people, places, or practices that bring you back to centre. Maybe it's a chat with a supportive friend, a quick binge of your favourite feel-good TV show, or a walk in the park where the only drama comes from squirrels chasing each other. Find your anchors and hold onto them.

Practical Strategies to Outsmart Negativity

Now that we've identified the obstacles, let's tackle them head-on with a few practical (and surprisingly simple) strategies:

Gratitude Journaling

Write down three things you're grateful for each day. Yes, even on bad days. (Hint: Coffee counts. So does indoor plumbing.)

Mindfulness Moments

Pause and notice the world around you. The smell of fresh bread, the sound of birds chirping, or the feel of a warm mug in your hands – mindfulness is all about soaking in the little things.

Reframe the Negative

Caught in a spiral of negativity? Ask yourself, Is there another way to look at this? Sometimes, a shift in perspective is all it takes.

Connect with Positivity

Surround yourself with uplifting people, books, or podcasts. (And if you're short on people, a video of a baby panda rolling down a hill works wonders.)

Focus on One Small Step

Feeling overwhelmed? Choose one thing – just one – to tackle. Sometimes, taking that first step is all you need to feel like you're back in control.

Progress, Not Perfection

Positivity isn't about getting it right all the time. Life is messy, complicated, and occasionally involves stepping on a LEGO barefoot. But every small choice to focus on the good is a step toward a more positive life.

So, the next time negativity sneaks in, remind yourself: it's not about avoiding the bad – it's about finding the good, even in the middle of it all. And who knows? Maybe that tiny shift in focus is all you need to turn your day around.

Go ahead, give it a try. After all, you've got nothing to lose – and maybe a lot of joy to gain.

CHAPTER THIRTEEN

The Seven Switches: Quick Wins and Simple Tips

Let's make this easy, shall we? Here's a rundown of the seven switches, complete with bite-sized tips to help you switch them on with minimal fuss (and maybe even a smile).

1. The Appreciation Switch

Key Idea: Look for the good in your life – even the little things. Gratitude gives your brain a nudge in the right direction, helping you focus on positivity instead of potholes.

Quick Tip: At the end of the day, jot down three things you're grateful for. Think small – a decent Wi-Fi signal, a really good biscuit, or finding matching socks (a modern miracle).

2. The Mindfulness Switch

Key Idea: Stay present. Mindfulness is the art of focusing on the here and now, which is far more productive than obsessing over that awkward thing you said in 2008.

Quick Tip: Feeling frazzled? Take a minute to breathe deeply. Inhale... hold... exhale. Bonus points if you're holding a cup of tea while you do it – it's practically a mindfulness double score.

3. The Kindness Switch

Key Idea: Kindness doesn't just make the world brighter; it also makes you feel amazing. Even the smallest act of compassion can ripple out in ways you'd never expect.

Quick Tip: Commit to one act of kindness today. Compliment someone, hold the door, or just smile at a stranger (yes, even if they look grumpy – it's worth a shot).

4. The Self-Belief Switch

Key Idea: Confidence isn't something you're born with – it's something you build. Start with small wins, and watch your belief in yourself grow stronger with each step.

Quick Tip: Write down one thing you've done well recently. Maybe you aced a work project or finally folded the laundry. Whatever it is, own it – you did that!

5. The Perspective Switch

Key Idea: Challenges aren't just roadblocks – they're lessons in disguise. (Sneaky, I know.) Change how you view setbacks, and you'll find opportunities where you least expect them.

Quick Tip: The next time life takes an unexpected turn, pause and ask, "What's one good thing I can take from this?" Even if the answer is just, "I learned what not to do," that's progress.

6. The Resilience Switch

Key Idea: Resilience isn't about avoiding difficulties; it's about bouncing back when life gets messy. Think of it as your emotional superpower.

Quick Tip: Reflect on a time when you overcame a challenge. What got you through it? Write it down – you've done it before, and you can do it again.

7. The Visualization Switch

Key Idea: Dream big, but dream clearly. Visualisation isn't just daydreaming; it's a tool to focus your energy and align your actions with your goals.

Quick Tip: Spend five minutes today picturing what success looks like for you. The clearer your vision, the easier it is to work toward it.

And there you have it! Your seven switches, all neatly packaged with quick, actionable tips. Keep this guide handy – it's like a portable positivity toolkit, ready to help you light up your day whenever you need it.

CHAPTER FOURTEEN

Cheat Sheet for Switching On Positivity

Let's face it, some days just don't go to plan. Whether it's spilled coffee, endless emails, or the universe deciding to test your patience, positivity can feel as elusive as the last biscuit in the tin. That's where this cheat sheet comes in – a quick, no-nonsense guide to switching on the right mindset when you need it most.

When You Need to Switch On…

Feeling stuck?

Give the Appreciation Switch a whirl. Take a moment to notice the good, whether it's your favourite cup of tea or the fact you didn't burn the toast this morning. It's the small wins that count.

Overwhelmed?

Time to activate the Mindfulness Switch. Pause, breathe, and focus on what's right in front of you. Forget tomorrow's to-do list – today's cup of coffee deserves your full attention.

Low on energy?

Flip the Kindness Switch. Even the tiniest act, like smiling at someone or holding a door, can give you a surprising energy boost. It's positivity with a side of feel-good.

Doubting yourself?

Switch on Self-Belief. Think about one thing you've accomplished recently – even if it's managing to keep a plant alive for longer than a week. You're doing better than you think!

Frustrated by setbacks?

Cue the Perspective Switch. Step back and ask, "What can I learn from this?" Sometimes the detour is where the best stories happen (even if it doesn't feel like it at the time).

Facing challenges?

Call up the Resilience Switch. Remind yourself of a tough time you got through before. If you handled that, you can handle this. Resilience is your secret superpower.

Lacking direction?

Time for the Visualisation Switch. Picture where you want to go and what success looks like. A clear mental map is half the journey sorted.

A Pocket Reminder

Life's not about avoiding the tough days – it's about knowing you've got the tools to handle them. Keep this cheat sheet close, whether it's taped to your fridge, tucked in your journal, or pinned to your office wall. Because when life dims the lights, you've got the switches to brighten your perspective and steer the day back on course.

Remember: you've got this.

CHAPTER FIFTEEN

Bonus Section: Staying Positive in a Divided World

Let's face it: navigating the world of differing opinions can feel like stepping into a minefield. One minute you're scrolling through the news with your morning coffee, and the next, you're clutching the mug a little too tightly, wondering how someone could possibly think that way. It's enough to make you want to scream – or at least turn off your Wi-Fi and live in a cave.

But before we retreat to the wilderness, let's explore how to keep our cool and stay positive when faced with opinions that make us want to fling the nearest cushion at the TV. Spoiler alert: it's not about agreeing with everyone (thank goodness) but about finding peace amid the chaos.

1. Pause Before Reacting

When you hear or read something that riles you up, take a deep breath. No, really – stop everything, inhale for four counts, hold for four counts, and exhale for four counts. There's something magical about pausing. It gives your brain time to process and reminds your hands not to write a scathing reply (however satisfying it might feel in the moment).

Think of this pause as the emotional equivalent of looking both ways before crossing the road. It could save you from an angry rant you'll cringe about later.

2. Channel Your Inner Detective

Instead of dismissing someone's view outright, approach it with curiosity. What might have led them to this perspective? What life experiences, upbringing, or values shaped their thinking?

No, this doesn't mean you need to agree with them, but seeing the human behind the opinion can soften your frustration. It's like discovering the villain in a movie had a tragic backstory. You might still disagree with their methods, but at least you understand where they're coming from.

3. Control the Controllables

Here's the thing: you can't change how someone else thinks. (Trust me, I've tried, and the results weren't pretty.) What you can do is focus on what's within your power – your actions, your choices, and your contributions to the world.

Feeling angry about injustice? Volunteer, donate, or advocate for change. Annoyed by negativity online? Share something uplifting instead. Every small action you take aligns you with your values and shifts your focus from frustration to empowerment.

4. Unplug (and Replug Somewhere Better)

If the news or social media is draining your positivity faster than a hole in a bucket, it's time to step away. This doesn't mean burying your head in the sand; it means protecting your peace.

Go for a walk, read a book, or watch videos of puppies falling over. (Seriously, it's hard to stay mad when there's a clumsy Labrador on your screen.) When you come back to the world of opinions, you'll feel refreshed and less like screaming into the void.

5. Practice the Art of Kindness (Yes, Even Now)

Here's a challenge: the next time someone's opinion makes you see red, silently wish them well. Not sarcastically, but genuinely. Say to yourself, "I hope they find peace and clarity."

It's hard to stay angry when you're extending kindness, even silently. Plus, it reminds you that we're all just humans doing the best we can with what we know.

6. What's the Real Trigger Here?

Anger often says more about us than the person we're angry at. Take a moment to ask, Why does this bother me so much?

Maybe it clashes with a deeply held value, or perhaps it touches on a fear or insecurity. Understanding the root of your frustration can help you address it constructively rather than letting it fester.

7. Balance the Scales with Positivity

For every frustrating opinion you encounter, find something uplifting to balance it out. A story of kindness, a moment of progress, or even a silly meme that makes you laugh. It's like an emotional seesaw – positivity on one side, negativity on the other. The goal isn't to ignore the heavy stuff but to make sure it doesn't weigh you down completely.

Quote for Thought:

"We don't have to agree with everyone, but we can choose how we respond. And in that choice lies our peace."

Takeaway Reflection:

You can't control the world's opinions, but you can control how they affect you. By approaching differences with curiosity, compassion, and a focus on your own actions, you'll find it easier to stay grounded and positive – even when opinions clash.

So, the next time you feel your blood pressure rising at the news or a social media post, remember this: you've got your switches, you've got your tools, and you've got the power to protect your peace. Now go out there and spread a little light – because the world could always use more of it.

CHAPTER SIXTEEN

Shine on: Over to you

Well, here we are – at the end of the book, but hopefully just the beginning of your positivity journey. If you've made it this far, first of all, bravo! Not everyone takes the time to invest in themselves like this. You've done something wonderful for yourself, and I think that deserves a little celebration. Go on, give yourself a pat on the back (or a piece of cake – I'm not judging).

Now that you've got your positivity toolkit filled with switches, you're ready to light up your life, even on those days when everything feels a bit foggy. Whether it's the Gratitude Switch, the Perspective Switch, or any of the others, each one is there to help you bring a little more light into the world – and, let's be honest, we could all use more of that.

It's All in Your Hands

Here's the thing about light switches: they're simple to use, but you're the only one who can flick them. Sure, life might try to convince you the bulb's gone out or that the wiring's faulty, but trust me, the power's there, and it's all yours. The goal isn't perfection – this isn't a competition for the World's Most Positive Person (though I hear the trophy would be very shiny). Instead, it's about progress: those little moments of light you choose to create every day.

Your Next Step

Now that you've got the tools, the real fun begins: putting them to use. Start small – maybe write down one thing you're grateful for today, take five deep breaths to reset, or reframe that mildly infuriating situation (yes, I mean the one involving that person who never signals at roundabouts).

A Final Thank You

Before you go, I just want to say thank you. Thank you for picking up this book, for trusting me to guide you, and for committing to your own growth. Writing this book has been a joy, and knowing it might make even the tiniest difference in your life? Well, that's the cherry on top.

A Parting Thought

Let me leave you with this little nugget: Life doesn't have to be perfect to be beautiful. Sometimes, it's the quirks, the surprises, and even the challenges that bring the brightest light.

So, here's to you – flicking your switches, shining your light, and making the world a brighter place, one moment at a time. When things get dark (as they sometimes do), remember: you've got everything you need to turn the light back on.

Now, go out there and shine on. The next chapter of you is waiting to be written – and I've got a good feeling it's going to be brilliant.

Ready to Take the Next Step?

If The Positivity Switch has inspired you to bring more joy, clarity, and resilience into your life, why not continue the journey with Switch Your Light On: A Guided Journal for Everyday Positivity?

This beautifully designed journal is the perfect companion to help you put the seven switches into practice. Packed with engaging prompts, creative exercises, and space for personal reflections, it's a hands-on way to deepen your positivity journey.

1. Explore and reflect: Dive into guided activities to bring each switch to life.

2. Get creative: Use doodle-friendly pages to map out your thoughts and ideas.

3. Stay motivated: Track your progress and celebrate your wins along the way.

Start transforming your mindset one page at a time. Grab your copy of Switch Your Light On today and let your positivity shine even brighter!